REASON WHY ADVERTISING

sound wisdom.
Porque tu éxito importa

ORIGINAL CLASSIC EDITION

REASON WHY ADVERTISING

FROM THE FATHER OF ADVERTISING AS SALESMANSHIP-IN-PRINT

JOHN E. KENNEDY

First published in 1914 by John E. Kennedy.

Reprint edition by Sound Wisdom, 2025

ISBN 13 TP: 978-1-64095-648-3

ISBN 13 eBook: 978-1-64095-649-0

1 2 3 4 5 6 7 8 / 29 28 27 26 25

CONTENTS

CHAPTER 1

YOU MUST DO THE SUM TO PROVE IT

Advertising should be judged *only* by the goods it is conclusively known to sell at a given cost. Mere opinions on advertising copy should be excluded from consideration.

Opinions on advertising are as conflicting as opinions on religion. Forty percent of all the people in the world are Buddhists, and are of the opinion that Buddhism is the only true religion. Twelve percent of the world's people, being Roman Catholics, are firm in the opinion that the remaining 88 percent are wrong, and sure of damnation accordingly.

Eight percent of the world's people being Protestants believe that both the Buddhists and the Catholics, and all others, are deplorably ignorant of the only true faith, which of course must be their own particular sect of Protestantism. And neither Buddhist, Catholic, nor Protestant can convince the 2 percent of Jews that their opinion is wrong and should be changed.

This is a sidelight on the inconsistency of mere opinion.

Religion must continue in the realm of *opinion*, because no one can decide which creed is right and which wrong till they die and find out the facts for themselves. And no mere human who died has ever come back to earth to settle the dispute.

But it is different with advertising, as it is with mechanics or with medicine, all three of which can be conclusively *tested*.

Many advertisers, however, seem satisfied to spend their money on mere opinions about advertising when they might have invested it on evidence about advertising. These are the advertisers whose business must die before they can be convinced that "general publicity" (merely "keeping the name before the people") is wrong and "salesmanship on paper" right.

They blindly gamble in advertising when they might have safely *invested* in it. If they were to buy any other kind of service, except advertising, they would demand tangible proof of its efficacy before they spent money on it.

If they hired a salesperson, for instance, they would expect them to prove they were earning their salary by making a satisfactory record on sales. They would not accept, for long, statements that they were "making a general impression on the trade" for their salary.

Nor would they be satisfied with the statement that they were "keeping the name before the people" profitably enough to compensate for lack of sales.

Nor would they enthuse over a report that they were "influencing sales" for their other salespeople. What the advertising employer would demand from the salesperson would be profitable *orders*. They would demand *sales*, clearly made by the salesperson themselves, each sale carrying a given profit over cost for the employer.

That is just what the advertising employer should demand from their advertising expenditure, too: sales—proven sales—carrying a satisfactory profit. And if they insist upon it, they can get the kind of advertising which will actually produce sales instead of a vague "general influence on sales."

Because true advertising is only "salesmanship on paper" after all. When it is anything less than salesmanship, it is not _real_ advertising, but only _general publicity_. And general publicity admittedly claims only to "keep the name before the people," to produce a "general impression on the trade," and to "influence sales" for the salespeople.

It makes the same lame excuses as would be made by a salesperson who failed to earn their salary in actually _selling_ goods. But general publicity, or any other advertising, should be judged by the selfsame standards as the salesperson is judged—by the goods it is clearly proven to _sell_ at a given cost per dollar invested in it.

✻ advertising should be Judged only by the goods it is conclusively known to Sell at a given Cost ✻

CHAPTER 2

TO WHOM ARE YOU ADVERTISING?

M r. Advertiser! You spend your money to tell people what you've got to sell.

Now, what kind of people can afford to buy your particular goods?

What income must they possess to be probable consumers of *your* advertised product? How many possibilities of sale has your product per thousand average readers?

These are all vital factors in the framing up of your campaign, and in the prospects of success from it. Here are some census figures upon which we base our campaigns and calculations.

In the year 1900 there were 15,964,000 families in the United States. These families averaged about five persons each, or a total population of 75,994,575. Fifty-one percent of that population lived in the country; 10⅔ percent was semi-urban; and 38⅓ percent lived in cities and towns.

The newspapers and periodicals these families read had a total circulation of 8,168,148,749 copies per year. That means 512 copies per year per family, or nearly *two copies per day* for each family.

A great deal of reading, isn't it?

Now comes the astonishing part of the census figures. Nearly 33 percent of all these families had an average income of less than $400 per year, or about $80 per capita.

Only 21 percent of these families had an annual income of $400 to $600. Only 15 percent of these families had an annual income of $600 to $900. Only 10½ percent of them had an annual income of $900 to $1,200. Only 7½ percent of them had an annual income of $1,800 to $3,000.

And, of the automobile class only 5 percent had an income of over $3,000 per family, or $600 per capita.

Now, wouldn't that set you thinking?

Suppose you have pianos to sell through advertising. How many families of the total that read newspapers and magazines could afford to buy one? Then, how many of these are already supplied?

That estimate shows your *possible market* through advertising, and indicates the way that market must be approached.

It also shows about how many readers you must pay to reach who cannot buy your piano, no matter how much your advertising makes them want it. And it also shows the futility of writing "catchy" copy to attract the greatest number of readers for your advertisement. What you need is not numbers of readers, but class of readers. That very limited class you must convince, when you once get its attention, or you lose all profit from your piano advertising.

You must make up in conviction and selling force for what you lose in possible number of purchasers with such a proposition.

But when your product is something which can be used by the masses, it is then a better subject for advertising. Because you then have about 85 percent more possibilities of sale, among average readers, than you would have had with a piano or automobile. The current mistake in advertising to this great 85 percent

WHAT YOU NEED IS NOT NUMBERS OF READERS, BUT CLASS OF READERS.

of average families is that of talking over their heads in terms and thought forms which are unfamiliar or unintelligible to them.

Observe that not one of this great 85 percent of families has an income of more than $1,800 a year, or $360 per person. Observe also that the average income of this great 85 percent is less than $500 per year, per family, or $100 per head. We must not expect the average of such people to have classical educations, nor an excessive appreciation of art and inference.

Neither are they as children in intellect, nor thick-headed fools. They are just average Americans of good average intelligence, considerable shrewdness, and large bumps of incredulity. Most of them might have come "from Missouri" because they all have "show me!" ever ready in their minds, when any plausible advertising claim is made to them.

But they are willing to be "shown" when the arguments are sensible enough, as well as *simple* enough, to appeal readily to their mental makeup. They are not suffocating for want of pretty pictures and pleasing phrases in advertising.

What they are most interested in is, "Show me how to get more for my money of what I *need* for existence and comfort rather than for luxury." This "great 85 percent" of readers has a peculiar habit of thought or mental caliber of its own which responds most freely to a certain well-defined form of approach and reasoning.

To strike the responsive chord with the class of readers aimed at is to multiply the selling power of every reason why given and every line of space used. So a few pointers upon this will be in order for our next chapter.

CHAPTER 3

THE RESPONSIVE CHORD IN ADVERTISING

Advertising is just salesmanship on paper. It is a means of multiplying by several thousandfold the work of the salesperson who writes it.

With the salary paid to a single salesperson it is possible, through advertising, to reach a thousand customers for every one he could have reached orally.

It is also a means of discovering and developing *new* customers where they were not previously known to exist. These facts are mentioned here because few businesspeople have a correct idea of what true advertising should consist of.

To start with the wrong point of view on an advertising campaign is to grope, experiment, and speculate, with an appropriation which should have been *invested* as intelligently as in merchandise.

True advertising is just salesmanship multiplied. When we multiply nothing by ten thousand we still have nothing as a result. When we multiply a pretty picture, or a catchphrase, or the mere name of a firm or article a thousand times we have comparatively nothing as a result.

But when we multiply one thousand times a good, strong, clearly expressed *reason why* a person should buy the article we want to sell, we then have impressed, through advertising, one thousand more people with that reason than if it had been told verbally to one person by the same salesperson.

Of course, cold type usually lacks the personal influence of the salesperson and, because of this, even salesmanship on paper needs to be stronger–more convincing and conclusive than salesmanship need be by word of mouth.

Besides, when we multiply anything a thousand-fold, at a large expense for the mechanical process of doing so, it is wisdom to see that the thing to be multiplied is as nearly perfect as we can get it.

TRUE ADVERTISING IS JUST SALESMANSHIP MULTIPLIED.

Nothing multiplied by one thousand costs just the same for the mechanical expense of multiplying it, but the net result is nothing–less that expense. This is why so many advertising campaigns fail. Because the good folks who spend their money for space have no definite idea of what should occupy it.

When we clearly understand that salesmanship alone should fill it, we all know, in a general way, what that means, though each of us might go about it in a different way. *Salesmanship on paper* means convincing readers that they should buy the article we want to sell.

Many good salespeople find it impossible to do this "convincing on paper" because the customer does not stand before them, with their facial expression as an index to the line of talk the salesperson should use in that particular case.

This is where the creative power of the salesperson on paper becomes vitally necessary. They must, first of all, analyze the proposition thoroughly–master the full details of the thing to be sold, then lay out a strong logical line of argument upon it, "lime-lighting" the good points and subtly masking the bad ones out of the reader's mental vision.

SALESMANSHIP ON PAPER MEANS CONVINCING READERS THAT THEY SHOULD BUY THE ARTICLE WE WANT TO SELL.

All this, however, is just what any good salesperson on the road or in the warehouse could, should, and probably does do. But a glance at the advertising pages of current publications will show how comparatively few advertisers adopt these first principles of salesmanship in their copy. However, it is after this that the true genius and power of the able salesperson on paper must be exerted. That consists in the staging of the arguments to fit the audience.

A given argument, presented in a certain form of thought and expression, will strike responsively in the minds of a given number, among the class of people aimed at, in each thousand.

If that percent be high, it means large profit to the advertiser–large returns. If that percent be low, it means that the advertisement has not convinced, has not struck responsively upon the particular class for whom the article advertised is best adapted, notwithstanding the sound argument used. This peculiarly "responsive" quality in an advertisement may be called its personality.

Observe that it need not be the personality of the writer at all, but the personality which he estimates will best fit the particular class of people who compose the largest field of sale for the article advertised.

This intangible personality feature may be likened to the keynote of a church or of a music hall. It is well known that every such building will respond most fully (in sound) to some one particular musical note of the scale, in proportion to the interior size and shape of the structure. This, a note which sounds full, clear, and vibrant in one such edifice, will sound thin, flat, and harsh in another. Because it is not the *responsive chord* of the second building as it is of the first.

The musician who could look at the inside of a church, then declare its responsive chord from an estimate, would be in kindred position to the advertising writer who could most profitably fit the personality of his reason-why salesmanship to the class he aims at.

To strike the responsive chord full and true with that class would mean 100 percent in possible results, from the arguments deduced. To strike a chord which sounded harsh, uncongenial, or unfamiliar to that class, would be to arouse latent antagonism or distrust. Either of these would discount the effect of the same logic, from 25 to 50 percent.

That is why the successful salesperson on paper must possess imagination as well as logic. He must be able to form a clear conception of the class he aims to convince. He must estimate how the average mind of

<u>that class is likely to work under a certain argument,</u> <u>and under a certain mode of expressing it.</u>

Then, he must be able to create the personality, in his mode of expression, which will strike the most responsive chord with the greatest possible number.

Some few advertisers possess this power of creating a personality which fits responsively the mass of humanity–the great 85 percent. And this ability to estimate the average mentality, the habit of thought, of the class aimed at, with the power to create a personality in the copy which will fit it most agreeably and familiarly, is what the reason-why salesperson on paper must have, in addition to the logical arguments of the salesperson in any other field.

The difference in results between copy written by two equally bright people may be, and often is, 80 percent, though the same space be used in each case to sell the selfsame article. That difference consists, first of all, in the quality of argument, the "reason why" that each of the two lines of copy contains, and next in the personality with which these arguments have been invested, in either copy, so as to strike the most responsive chord with the class of readers aimed at.

The faculty of taking the mental measure of a given class and gauging their habit of thought is a sort

THE SUCCESSFUL SALESPERSON ON PAPER MUST POSSESS IMAGINATION AS WELL AS LOGIC.

of instinct, such as guides the timber explorer, who travels a hundred square miles of forest and estimates closely just how many thousand feet of timber are on it, though he never counts a tree.

That sales of timber lands running into millions of dollars have been regularly made on this instinctive knowledge of a single person is evidence of the general accuracy, and reliability, of such trained and instinctive estimates. This same faculty has more to do with successful salesmanship on paper than is generally recognized. And it is rare enough to be interesting.

CHAPTER 4

LET THERE BE LIGHT

Now, let us be frank! Let us look at this subject of advertising squarely and dissect it. Let us discard all prejudice or predilection and accept only *evidence* in our final investigation.

Let us cut out sentiment, precedent, and "popular opinion," and treat the subject as though we had never heard of it before and "came from Missouri." If, for instance, we had a load of hay to sell, how would we attempt to sell it?

Would we show our customers the daisies that grew in it, ask them to note the style of the loading, the fine pair of horses that draw it, and the Van Dyke beard of the driver? Would we tell them this is the same kind of hay as was raked by "Maud Muller on a summer's day" in Whittier's poem?

Guess not!

We'd tell them of the nutritious qualities that particular load of hay possessed for the feeding of horses, and then we'd name the price delivered, show why the hay was worth it, and let it go at that.

Now, if our customer lived at a distance, and we must sell him the hay by letter, how would we proceed? Quote "Maud Muller" to him, then refer to the daisies, the horses, the beard? No, sir—not for a moment! We would confine ourselves carefully to the feeding qualities of our hay and to the advantages of buying while the price was right.

But suppose we had five hundred loads of this hay to sell, instead of one load, and did not know just where to write to in order to sell it.

That's when we'd *advertise!* But does the fact of our going into print mean that we *must* go into literature, art, or clever conceits in space-filling too, in order to sell our hay through advertising?

Are we not still trying to sell just horse feed? How can we expect the picture of "Maud Muller on a summer's day" to help us close a deal with an unpoetical party who has horses to feed and who must do it economically?

The horse owner knows good hay when he sees it, and he will know it from description almost as well as from sight.

When he needs good hay, then the most *interesting* thing we can tell him is a description of the hay we have to sell, and why it is good, and why it is worth the price. No amount of Maud Muller pictures or "association of ideas" will sell him hay so surely and quickly as plain hay-talk and horse-sense.

But the advertiser will be told that "in order for an advertisement to sell goods it must first be seen and read!" He will also be told that "in the mass of reading matter surrounding your advertisement your space must be made more *attractive* than the rest, in order to be seen and read by the largest possible number."

Now, at first sight this line of talk looks logical enough, but how does it dissect? Suppose you have a pretty Maud Muller advertisement about your hay, with a fancy border of daisies all around it, and a delicate vignette of "the judge looked back as he climbed the hill!"

You would certainly attract the attention of many more readers with that ad than with the bald caption of "hay delivered at $8.00 a ton." But the person who *wants hay* is the only party you can get back the cost of your advertising from, and you can interest him more intensely with the hay caption than with all the "Maud Muller" kind of ads in the publication field.

You can afford to lose the "attention" of 400,000 readers who have no use for hay if you can clinch sales for your five hundred loads with the few people who do need it.

Observe that it is not necessary to "attract the attention" of *every* reader in a 430,000 circulation in order to sell 500 loads of hay. But it is vitally necessary that you convince at least five hundred probable purchasers that you have the kind of hay they need at the price they can afford to pay for it.

If an advertisement in a circulation of 430,000 costs $60 and we have a profit of $1.00 per load on hay, we need only sell one load each to sixty people in order to pay expenses.

But if we "attract the attention" of 80,000 people by our advertisement and sell only thirty loads of hay to them, we would then be out $30 and must credit the balance of our advertising investment to general publicity—to "keeping the name before people" etc.—in the vague hope that some other day these people may perhaps buy hay from us, if we then have it to sell.

YOU CAN AFFORD TO LOSE THE "ATTENTION" OF 400,000 READERS WHO HAVE NO USE FOR HAY IF YOU CAN CLINCH SALES FOR YOUR FIVE HUNDRED LOADS WITH THE FEW PEOPLE WHO DO NEED IT.

That mistaken idea of attracting the attention of the greatest number for a given price is what costs fortunes to advertisers annually. The striving to "attract attention" instead of striving to positively sell goods is the basis of all advertising misunderstanding.

So long as "attracting attention" remains the aim of advertisers, so long will the process of attracting it remain in the hands of advertising people who affect the literary and artistic attitude, rather than the plain, logical, convincing attitude of the reason-why salesperson on paper. And great are the advertising writers' temptations to use "attractive" copy at the expense of convincing copy. Because great is the temptation to be considered "smart," "bright," "catchy," "literary," "artistic," "dignified," "high-grade," etc.

There is popular applause for the writer of catchy general publicity, which attracts attention even though it does not sell goods. But there is no applause for the writer of prosaic salesmanship on paper which is forceful enough and convincing enough to actually *sell* goods in volume. This is one reason why "catchy" advertising is so current, and true reason-why salesmanship in type so rare.

Another reason is the far greater cost to produce studied reason-why salesmanship in type than to produce four times as much catchy general publicity.

A still further reason is that the makers of general publicity know they can never be *held to account* for definite results from the latter kind of copy, because nothing definite is promised through it.

- To "keep the name before the people."

- To "make a general impression on the trade."

- To "influence sales."

- To "protect the market."

These are the vague nothings promised to the advertiser by the makers of general publicity. These are the fractional parts of advertising he gets in return for an outlay which could have brought him back 150 percent instead of 30 to 90 percent of his outlay for space.

Remember that reason-why salesmanship on paper will do all that general publicity can do toward "keeping the name before the people," "creating a general impression on the trade," etc.

And, in addition to this, it can actually, positively, and conclusively *sell goods* through retailers (or by mail) in sufficient volume to pay 50 to 300 percent profit on the investment in space it occupies.

THE MAKERS OF
GENERAL PUBLICITY
KNOW THEY CAN NEVER
BE HELD TO ACCOUNT
FOR DEFINITE RESULTS
FROM THE LATTER KIND
OF COPY, BECAUSE
NOTHING DEFINITE IS
PROMISED THROUGH IT.

CHAPTER 5

THEY WHO BLINDLY FOLLOW THE BLIND

Carlyle compared humankind to a flock of sheep. He said, "Stretch a rope across a country path, about a foot and a half from the ground. Then drive a flock of sheep over it! When the bellwether (or leader) has jumped that elevated rope, lower it to the ground and note what happens."

Every sheep in the flock that follows will jump a foot and a half in the air over that same rope, though it now lies slack on the earth. They follow the bellwether blindly, unreasoningly, without regard to changed conditions. They don't jump for the same reason that the bellwether jumped, but because they saw another sheep jumped a given height at a given spot.

Carlyle's comparison fits the advertising situation like a blister. There be flocks of sheep innumerable in the advertising field, neighbor! When Sapolio (the soap manufacturer) used the "Spotless Town" jingles merely to revive mental impressions created by previous logical advertising, the flock of sheep ran amuck on jingles, regardless of the application to other purposes.

When "Uneeda Biscuit" appeared on the market to fill a colossal waiting demand for a five-cent package, it was backed by an appropriation the mere volume of which must create a sensation with retailers (whether it actually sold goods to consumers or not).

This, in turn, was followed by a brood of inane trademarks launched on the advertising field after it and because of it. When Ivory soap publicity appeared on the scene, with its full pages of pretty pictures, and its 5 percent of selling effect, the sheep concluded that, too, must be "the best ever" in advertising, so they promptly got in line and leaped the imaginary rope.

Then we had an epidemic of empty catchphrases, following hard upon "Good morning! Have you used Pear's soap?" This, regardless of the fact that Pear's much parodied phrase had a foundation of a hundred years in accumulated advertising to tide it over its period of mental aberration.

Where are these false gods of advertising today?

"Spotless Town" is off the map, and Sapolio is now being advertised on the good old reason-why basis that built the company. The old-time brood of jingles and such other Uneeda chickens has gone home to roost long before the tolling of curfew bell.

"Uneeda Biscuit" itself, with the millions of trust money behind it, can keep up the publicity bluff better than it can afford to admit the mistake of starting it. But there are unwilling admissions of a change of heart in such of their advertisements as "The Food Value of a Soda Cracker," and other recent "type" copy. Where is that meteor of general publicity, "the Cremo Cigar," which one time flashed across the horizon of advertising, with its million-dollar outlay for billboard display in newspaper space?

It, too, has gone into eclipse.

Study the Ivory soap advertising of the present and watch it for the future. You will find in it, month by month, less pointless picture and more "reason why," though its advertising sponsors will hate to admit the change of attitude their later experience has compelled.

Pear's soap no longer says "good morning" nor quotes, in place of it, any other catchphrase. Yet their once famous line is enshrined forever in the minds of old fogy advertising people, who swear by the Pear's catchphrase but who never buy Pear's soap as a result of it.

Meantime such stars in the firmament of general publicity have lighted the way to ruin for a few dozen flocks of sheep who thought they were following reliable "bellwethers" when they were only following fads.

And every new fad, started in a large way by any big advertiser (who has money enough to burn a big bluff, and pride enough to sustain that bluff till he can quietly change his play), will be applauded, copied, and "advised" by those who do not themselves understand the compass, and so must follow the lead of others as incapable as themselves.

But is there, you ask, any reliable compass by which an advertiser's ship may be safely steered to success? There is, reader, a guide practically as reliable to the advertiser as is the compass to the mariner. Its guidance in not based upon mere opinion, nor on guesswork, nor on blind following of the blind. It is based upon carefully tabulated results derived from actual tests made with different kinds of copy, in different mediums, compared year after year on scores of different advertising propositions.

By this means the exact *earning power* of each piece of copy may be told by the number of inquiries it produced for a given cost, and the number of direct sales that resulted from the inquiries.

Not only this, but the relative earning power of *each* publication is thereby accurately revealed by the cost of inquiries and sales, through each particular medium in which the same copy is run without regard to mere circulation claims.

The results from any one mail order account using a given kind of copy might only indicate the effectiveness of that kind of copy for that particular article. This would afford no conclusive evidence as to how that kind of copy might work with a different sort of mail order proposition, or in general advertising. But when a given kind of copy produces almost a *uniform* kind of result for different mail order accounts, and does it *consistently* for years, it means something definite and indisputable to advertisers.

And when the same kind of copy is tried out in general advertising, for goods sold through retailers, with the same consistent sort of result (judged by records of comparative sales in different but equivalent territory), it, too, proves something definite and conclusive that advertisers cannot afford to ignore, no matter how

WHEN A GIVEN KIND OF COPY PRODUCES ALMOST A <u>UNIFORM</u> KIND OF RESULT FOR DIFFERENT MAIL ORDER ACCOUNTS, AND DOES IT <u>CONSISTENTLY</u> FOR YEARS, IT MEANS SOMETHING DEFINITE AND INDISPUTABLE TO ADVERTISERS.

partial they may be to their own pet fads in advertising or to friends in the advertising business.

CHAPTER 6

FORTUNES WASTED IN FOLLOWING WILL-O-THE-WISPS

K*eeping the name before the people* and *keeping everlastingly at it!* That, dear reader, is general publicity–a glory game under a convenient alias. Keeping the name before the people and keeping everlastingly at it may incidentally *influence* the sale of goods, providing no competing line is being actually advertised through reason-why salesmanship on paper.

But the main object of such general publicity may be less mercenary, more altruistic, than mere merchandising.

Attract attention. Interest the public with pretty pictures and cute catchwords. *Encourage the publisher* by paying him for plenty of unoccupied white space. Lastly, pay some agency a commission to spend the money with the least effort and the most fireworks. *That* is general publicity.

It is well enough, in its way, of course (like the Carnegie libraries). But what is here objected to is that some folks, who ought to know better, call this general publicity by the name of "advertising."

Now, advertising is, and should be, simply plebeian *salesmanship on paper*—a mere money making means of selling goods by the quickest and cheapest method.

There is no glory in the reason-why salesmanship on paper—no applause for it, no admiration—just *profit.*

Because it is simply common sense brought to bear directly upon the selling of goods. That is its province—just *selling goods* over the counter or by mail.

If you want to find out how few goods general publicity copy (keeping the name before the people) will actually sell, test some of what you are now using, in a mail order way—to sell goods, mark you (not merely to give away calendars or samples).

THERE IS NO GLORY IN THE REASON- WHY SALESMANSHIP ON PAPER—NO APPLAUSE FOR IT, NO ADMIRATION— JUST PROFIT.

That is the test that shatters advertising idols and dispels publicity illusions. You may have the smoothest catchphrase that ever happened–you may be thoroughly tickled with your witty wording, pretty platitudes, and artistic illustrations.

You may feel cocksure that you have a kind of advertising which couldn't fail (so long as the salespeople do its work in addition to their own). But suppose you should try to actually sell goods by mail with it.

If your world-beating advertisement, which "everybody sees" and admires, costs you $2.00 per inquiry, and if another kind of advertisement you don't like at all brings equally good inquiries, in the same space and same mediums, at 40 cents each, then you've learned something you can never afford to forget.

That is the kind of experience which makes one sit up and think hard before they recover from the jolt it gives them. And when they come to, they then see a great white light.

Under this new light some of the things they thought they knew before fade out into vapory "will-o'-the-wisps," and they long for things tangibly proven.

When they observe now a hoary "Old Ma" mail order advertisement that seems at first sight stupidly simple and countrified, they look twice into it to see if it isn't carefully loaded with hidden selling effect and subtle conviction under its guise of rural simplicity.

If they note it running for years without change, they no longer jump to the conclusion that the person who pays for it is merely a chump, serving his costly apprenticeship to our own guild of advanced advertisers.

No, they look closely at it now for the hallmarks of salesmanship, and where they find it running for months, without change of copy, they conclude there is some potent reason for it.

Because they then feel that, had *they* as sure a means of keeping tab on results as this mail order advertiser, they, too, might be using some "stale" copy in general advertising, instead of changing it often (without evidence) from bad to probably worse.

If they have tried over fifty different changes of copy that had pleased them better than the stale one, and had found (as others have done) that inquiries from them cost $1.20 to $2.90 each, they would be mighty glad to go back to the good old chestnut which produced inquiries regularly at 40 cents average.

They would look upon that ancient ad in the light of a tried and trusted friend. If they were asked to sell out their business, they might well appraise that bit of much-used ancient history at a price that would make many ad-smiths gasp. And why shouldn't they appraise it high up in the thousands?

If we spend $100,000 per year for space and fill that space with copy that costs $1.20 per inquiry (by mail, or over the counter), we get only 83,334 chances of sale out of our appropriation.

With the antique ad or its skillful equivalent, our $100,000 would have produced 250,000 inquiries at an average of 40 cents each.

These 250,000 inquiries would have cost us $300,000 to secure at $1.20 each. Why isn't the proven "40-cent" advertisement worth all it saves– $200,000 per year–so long as it continues to produce inquiries averaging 40 cents each, instead of at $1.20 each?

Well, why isn't such an advertisement worth more than the space it occupies each time it is published?

What is the "something" in a successful mail order advertisement that makes it pull equally good inquiries at a fraction of previous cost?

It is the same "something" that would make advertising sell goods over the retailer's counter, through general advertising, at correspondingly low cost.

WHY ISN'T SUCH
AN ADVERTISEMENT
WORTH MORE
THAN THE SPACE
IT OCCUPIES
EACH TIME IT IS
PUBLISHED?

That mysterious "something" is just printed persuasion, and its other name is *reason-why salesmanship in type*.

It is that sapient "something" which makes one advertiser rich in a few years, while lack of it ruins others who buy their space equally cheap, pay 5 percent less commission, and spend equally large appropriations. That "something" is "reason why" and conviction, saturated into the copy, so that the reader *must* believe the statements of merit thus claimed for the article.

Mere brilliance in advertising fails utterly to produce such profitable results (sales) if it lacks conviction. The seeing, admiring, or reading with interest of an advertisement by the public avails little in dollars and cents, to the person who pays for the space, if it fails to *convince* the public.

And that conviction can be imparted, without accident, at will, by the few advertising people who have closely studied the thought process through which conviction is induced, provided they have had the guiding light of experience with the facilities for comparing results obtained from a large variety of mail order copy.

These results have invariably shown that it is far better to repeat one single advertisement fifty times,

IT IS FAR BETTER TO REPEAT ONE SINGLE ADVERTISEMENT FIFTY TIMES, IF IT BE FULL OF CONVICTION, THAN TO PUBLISH FIFTY DIFFERENT ADVERTISEMENTS THAT LACK AS MUCH CONVICTION.

if it be full of conviction, than to publish fifty different advertisements that lack as much conviction, no matter how attractive, clever, or artistic, they may be.

In other words, one sound, convincing advertisement will sell more goods than fifty brilliant, catchy, strikingly displayed "ads" that have less conviction in them.

The only mission of true general advertising is to sell goods, by driving the people to the stores armed with such reasons and convictions that substitution will be difficult or impossible.

When advertising is not selling goods (through conviction), it is not doing as much as it can be made to do. So any advertiser who accepts mere general publicity or "keeping the name before the people" for his money, when he might have had all that and a positive selling force combined with it, is losing half the results he might have had from the same space filled with sound reason-why advertising.

ONE SOUND, CONVINCING ADVERTISEMENT WILL SELL MORE GOODS THAN FIFTY BRILLIANT, CATCHY, STRIKINGLY DISPLAYED "ADS" THAT HAVE LESS CONVICTION IN THEM.

CHAPTER 7

WHY SOME ADVERTISERS GROW WEALTHY WHILE OTHERS FAIL

Sixty percent of all new advertisers fail! Largely because they spend their money for space, under the delusion that space filled with anything "catchy" is advertising. They believe "money talks" in advertising, even when it says nothing.

They forget that space costs the same, whether we fill it with pictured nothings or with enduring convictions.

And the difference in results between two kinds of copy, costing the same for space in a single advertisement, has often exceeded 80 percent, as authenticated records on test cases prove.

SPACE COSTS THE SAME, WHETHER WE FILL IT WITH PICTURED NOTHINGS OR WITH ENDURING CONVICTIONS.

General advertisers, who have no means of tracing direct results and who spend their money for general publicity, may smile at this. But mail order advertisers know it is true. These are the kind of advertisers to whom advertising is not a blind speculation but systematic eyes-open *investment.*

Their records show the precise cost of every inquiry for their goods through advertising, because their every advertisement in every medium is separately keyed.

They can thus gauge accurately the relative *earning power* of each separate bit of copy published at their expense, and of each medium in which that copy has been inserted. They thus *know* what kind to avoid, as well as what kind to use. Please note that the current definition of general publicity is "keeping the name before the people."

When we speak of *general advertising*, we mean copy which sells goods through the retailer. (Note that general advertisers are *not* hereby advised to go into mail order business.) However, general advertising should possess as much positive selling force and conviction as it would need to actually and profitably sell goods direct by mail.

Here is the actual experience of a well-known national advertiser, who sells a $5.00 article by mail only.

This advertiser has proved that a certain fixed average percent of his inquiries convert into direct sales through his "follow-up" system. Each equally good inquiry is therefore worth a certain fixed price to him, which he can pay with profit.

One single piece of copy has been running for that advertiser (practically without change), in all mediums used, for over six years. Over $300,000 has been spent in repeated publication of that single bit of copy.

Why?

Because, it produced results (inquiries and sales) at lower cost than any other copy ever run for them in eight previous years. The first month inquiries from the best prior copy cost about 85 cents each.

Repetition of that copy for two years wore out some of its interest, so that inquiries from it finally cost an average of $1.85 each. New copy had been tried a great many times during the two-year interval, written by many different ad-smiths, but no other advertisement ever produced the inquiries at less than $1.85 average.

Some of the copy that looked good enough to try cost $14.20 per inquiry. And that was better looking copy than half of what fills general publicity space in costly mediums at this very minute. Consider what the knowledge derived from a large collection of certified

GENERAL ADVERTISING
SHOULD POSSESS AS
MUCH POSITIVE SELLING
FORCE AND CONVICTION
AS IT WOULD NEED
TO ACTUALLY AND
PROFITABLY SELL GOODS
DIRECT BY MAIL.

data, like the above, would mean if placed at the disposal of general advertisers who now "go it blind" on copy.

If the $5.00 article had been sold through retailers in the usual way, without accurate means of checking results from every advertisement, it is more than probable that the $14.20 kind of copy would have been used continuously. Because that was the catchy kind, so much in favor with general publicity advertisers. And it would have been considered good copy so long as the salespeople did its work, in addition to their own, the general results being credited in a general way to general publicity.

But it would clearly have required fourteen times as much of that "$14.20 kind" of alleged "advertising" to produce the same amount of *selling effect* upon the public as the 85-cent kind of copy (which averaged about $1.00 per inquiry over the two years) actually *did* produce.

Let us figure this out more conclusively: The Blank Company spent $75,000 per year for space, with copy producing inquiries at about $1.00 average.

It would thus have cost them about fourteen times as much, or $1,050,000 per year, to sell as many of their $5.00 articles through the $14.20 kind of "catchy" copy as it actually did cost them to sell the same quantity with the "$1.00-per-inquiry" kind of copy.

Good reader, get that thought clearly into your mind, for we're talking cold facts now. What was it worth to the Blank Company to get a new advertisement which would pull inquiries at the old rate of 85 cents each, when its most successful copy had worn out, after two years' use, so that inquiries were finally costing it $1.25 each on average?

Figure it out and you'll see that one single piece of such copy would be worth a third of their $75,000 yearly appropriation–inquiries for their goods and resulting sales. But "reason-why" copy did better than that, when applied on test.

It reduced the cost of inquiries, for the selfsame $5.00 article, to 41 cents average during the first two years it had been running. (It is still running, after six years' use.)

The earning power of every dollar *tripled* by the mere substitution of reason-why copy for the best copy the advertiser had used in eight years prior to that substitution.

An advertising appropriation of $75,000 made equal in proven earning power to what $225,000 would have

THE EARNING POWER OF EVERY DOLLAR TRIPLED BY THE MERE SUBSTITUTION OF REASON-WHY COPY.

earned with the copy which preceded it, and which was producing inquiries at $1.25.

That single piece of reason-why copy, which ran practically without change for about four months, had in that time produced approximately 60,976 inquiries. These were worth $1.25 each to the advertiser (or $91,464 in all), though their cost was reduced to 41 cents each, with an actual outlay of about $25,000.

In four months that one piece of copy had thus earned $66,466 more, for the advertiser, than the $1.25 kind of copy used immediately before it had produced from the same investment.

And what made it pull inquiries by mail is precisely what would make it produce inquiries verbally for the goods through retailers, by the use of intelligent *reason why* and conviction in the copy.

This is only one of many actual instances that could be cited.

CHAPTER 8

MAKING SURE OF RESULTS FROM GENERAL ADVERTISING

The first tangible return from the advertiser's money, when invested in space, (whether that space be filled with general advertising or with mail order advertising) is an inquiry for their goods.

That inquiry may be verbal to a clerk over the counter, or it may be by mail, in a written, stamped, and posted letter. But in either case, it is just an inquiry for the goods, of one sort or another. It is the first practical evidence that the money spent is earning something tangible in return.

Now, it may take twice or three times as much conviction in copy to make a consumer write an inquiry for goods, and post it, as it would have taken to make that same consumer inquire verbally for the goods advertised when passing a store that should sell them.

But when he does inquire verbally from a retailer, there are twice or three times as many chances of substitution, of "Don't keep it" or "Here's something better," as there would have been if that same consumer had written direct for it by mail.

Therefore, the advertisement which sends consumers to retailers should be as full of conviction as the successful mail order advertisement, in order to fortify that consumer against substitution: "Don't keep it," and "Here's something better."

Because if the advertisement fails to thus fortify the consumer with "reason why" and conviction, it may simply send him to the retail store to be switched on to a competing line of goods with which the retailer is heavily stocked, or which his clerks favor the sale of in preference to ours. In that case the advertising we pay for would sell goods for our non-advertising competitors.

Half the money spent to "keep the name before the people" results today in this substitution of non-advertised articles for the articles advertised through general publicity.

HALF THE MONEY SPENT TO "KEEP THE NAME BEFORE THE PEOPLE" RESULTS IN THE SUBSTITUTION OF NON-ADVERTISED ARTICLES FOR THE ARTICLES ADVERTISED THROUGH GENERAL PUBLICITY.

General publicity copy, when tested, is found in almost every case too weak to sell goods profitably by mail. And any copy which is not strong enough or convincing enough to sell goods by mail is not strong enough to make the consumer resist substitution, and the "Don't keep that kind" influence of retail conditions.

General advertising copy, to succeed profitably, must therefore cause not only a verbal inquiry for the goods, but must also have enough strong conviction saturated into it to make the consumer insist upon getting the goods he asks for, against probable substituting influence.

It must therefore give him better reason why he should buy our goods than he is likely to hear from the retail salesperson for the competing goods that salesperson may want to substitute.

And it must give him these "reasons why" in such lucid thought form that he can understand *without effort*, and so impressively that he will believe our reasoning claims. It must accomplish this in spite of his natural distrust of all advertisement statements.

This means that we must put into general advertising copy the precise qualities that would be necessary to sell goods profitably by mail. More than half the people who inquire for advertised goods out of curiosity as a result of general publicity (keeping the name before the people, etc.) *do not buy them* when they see them.

Because the competing goods look just as fine when shown and recommended by the substituting salesperson. The curiosity inquiry having no firm foundation of *reason why* under it cannot combat the personal influence of the salesperson.

This is why not more than a fourth of those who, out of mere curiosity, buy the first package through general publicity, ever buy the second or third consecutive package of the same article. Because they do not buy on conviction.

Meantime, it usually takes about all the profit in the first purchase of any generally advertised article to pay the cost of introducing it to the consumer's notice through advertising.

But with reason-why salesmanship on paper, results are insured and far more cumulative. Because a consumer need only be convinced once, through reason-why salesmanship on paper, that the article is what they should, for their own sake, buy and use.

When we thus convince them, we achieve more than fortifying them against substitution. We also help their imagination to find and recognize, in the article advertised, the very qualities claimed and proved for it in the copy. These qualities they might never have discovered for themselves, nor appreciated if they had casually discovered them in a mere "curiosity" purchase.

Because, through general publicity, their attention had only been *attracted*, not *compelled* and enduringly *impressed* with a logical understanding of these qualities.

But when once convinced in advance of purchase, through reason-why salesmanship in type, that the qualities claimed for the article do exist in them, they start using that article with a mental acceptance of these qualities. And because they begin using the article with an advance knowledge of, and belief in, its good points, their appreciation becomes permanent if the goods merit it.

They therefore make a second, third, and further consecutive purchases of the article as a result of having once read a single convincing reason-why advertisement about it.

This is where large and cumulative profits must come to the general advertiser—on the second, third, and *continued* purchases by readers of the first advertisement that reached their convictions.

These conviction qualities in copy are shown, by test, to be just as necessary in advertising design to sell

LARGE AND CUMULATIVE PROFITS COME TO THE GENERAL ADVERTISER ON THE SECOND, THIRD, AND <u>CONTINUED</u> PURCHASES.

goods profitably today, through retailers to consumers, as they are to sell goods direct by mail to consumers.

That is why every advertisement for goods to be sold through retailers (against substitution, and "Don't keep it" influences), should have as much positive selling force, reason why, and conviction in it as would be necessary to sell the goods by mail direct to consumers.

The difference in results from space in which this direct selling force of *reason why* has been used, and in results from similar space filled with general publicity, is often more than 60 percent. Conclusive tests on copy have clearly proved this, and a preceding article cites a vivid example of it from actual experience.

Any advertiser who uses mere general publicity when he might have all that and, in addition, a positive selling force combined with it is losing 50 percent to 80 percent of the results he might have had from the same identical appropriation.

Selling tests made on various kinds of copy and mediums have proved this for *reason why,* which is the heart and soul and essence of all good advertising.

CHAPTER 9

HOW MAIL ORDER ADVERTISING IS TESTED

Choose a list of reliable publications for a representative month's advertising. Run current copy in half the number of these publications for that month. Key each advertisement in each publication separately, so you will know just which advertisement and which publication each inquiry results from.

Then, run reason-why salesmanship in type copy in the remaining half of the publications, keying each advertisement separately, in each publication so you will know which advertisement and which medium each inquiry comes from.

By "keying" is meant that you change the reply address in each advertisement and in each publication.

Thus, in *Munsey's* you say "Address 86 State St."; in *Woman's World*, "75 State St."; and in *Wallaces Farmer* you say "6th floor 86 State St." while in another you say "8th floor 75 State St.," for instance. By arrangement with the post office all replies to these different addresses will be put into your letterbox, regardless of street address on envelope.

Now, you can tell by the envelope address on each reply or inquiry which publication and which particular piece of copy in that publication produced it.

Then, when the inquiries from the competing advertisements cease coming, you can total up the number of inquiries each publication produced from each particular advertisement.

Now, having the total number of inquiries from each individual advertisement in each medium, you divide that number into the cost of the space used for each piece of copy in each publication.

This will give you the exact cost, per inquiry, from each separate piece of copy in each publication. The cost per inquiry with your other current copy may then be intelligently compared with the cost per inquiry through reason-why salesmanship on paper.

Now, cross the copy for the second month's advertising test.

By this is meant–insert your other current copy, which appeared last month in *Munsey's,* in this month's *Wallaces Farmer,* for instance. And the *reason why* copy which appeared last month in *Woman's World* you now insert in *Munsey's* of this month. This gives a fair distribution of mediums to each competing advertisement.

When the inquiries cease coming from this second month's insertion, make the same record as before of cost per inquiry, for each piece of competing copy from each publication.

Then, add the total number of inquiries obtained from your other current copy during the same period. Then divide that total number into the total expenditure for space used in publication of that copy.

This will give the *average cost per inquiry*, with the kind of copy you have been regularly using.

Now, compare this with the *average cost per inquiry* obtained from the same publications, at the same identical periods, with *reason-why* results. The difference between the cost per inquiry with the two kinds of copy will then be a reliable index to the relative earning power of the two competing kinds of copy.

Now, use the same "follow-up" (booklets and letters) on all the inquiries from both sources.

The percentage of sales which results from each of the two competitive groups of inquiries and follow-up will then determine the relative profits to the advertiser from each kind of copy.

No test on earth can be more conclusive than this, and none is easier made. And what such a test reveals (in difference between results from two different kinds of copy) would stagger the average advertiser.

An extensive series of such tests, carried over a long period of time with many differing propositions, has proved a fine consistency in results.

It proved that the *reason-why* kind of advertising, which sold washing machines by mail at one third the cost other copy sold them, would, when applied according to the individual needs of the different articles, also sell violins, shoes, or pianos in about the same ratio.

Moreover, it has been found that the "something" in copy which sells these goods by mail (at one half to one third of the cost other copy sells them) will also sell them through retailers over the counter. That "something" is selling force–conviction–salesmanship saturated into the copy with sound *reasons why* as the foundation.

It is the salient "something" which makes millionaires of some advertisers in a few years, while other

NO TEST ON EARTH CAN BE MORE CONCLUSIVE THAN THIS, AND NONE IS EASIER MADE.

advertisers, spending the same amount of money for equally good propositions, go broke.

Now the kind of advertising which works these miracles of success may be the kind you personally like least—quite contrary to your preference in fact.

But advertising is not really intended to merely please the advertiser's fancy. Its first, last, and only duty is to sell goods for you, and to sell them at less cost than they can be sold without it.

The kind of advertising which will be found to do this at lowest cost is reason-why salesmanship on paper. Which is based not on what you like best to read but on what records prove will sell the most goods to readers per dollar of outlay.

SOUND <u>REASONS WHY</u> ARE THE SALIENT "SOMETHING" WHICH MAKES MILLIONAIRES OF SOME ADVERTISERS IN A FEW YEARS, WHILE OTHER ADVERTISERS GO BROKE.

CHAPTER 10

HOW TO TEST OUT GENERAL ADVERTISING

Select two cities of about the same population, in approximately the same climate, and with equally good newspapers. St. Paul and Minneapolis are fair examples, but scores of other equivalents can be named or chosen.

Check carefully the quantity of the advertised goods in these two cities which the retailers have on hand at a given date. Then ask them to keep record (on a blank form you supply) of the goods in your advertised lines which they stock within the next four months.

Then, run in one of the two competitive cities the general publicity you have already been using.

At the same time, run in the other competitive city *reason-why salesmanship on paper.* Spend for each kind exactly the same appropriation, and make it sufficiently liberal to show some results on the second month.

Continue this competitive copy for four months, which is the minimum time on which general advertising can be made to produce a fair measure of results.

Then, on a certain day, send out enough people to check the amount of the advertised goods in the hands of each retailer at the end of the four months.

Add to the total of goods on hand at the time of starting the test the goods since stocked in each city. Then subtract from this total the advertised goods remaining on the retailers' shelves, in each city, at end of the four months' advertising tests.

The difference between will show the quantity of your advertised goods actually sold to consumers, in each city, during the four months' period of actual selling test.

The difference between the value of goods sold in each city during the test period will then be a reliable index to the relative selling power of the two competing kinds of advertising used.

Now, cross the copy in each city for four months longer. Use *reason why* in the city where you previously used only current general publicity, and vice versa.

Check the goods on hand at end of the second four months again, as before. When you find the difference in sales (with the same expenditure for advertising) to be again heavily in favor of the reason-why copy (as in the first four months), you will have made a copy test that may save you over 25 percent to 50 percent of your national appropriation *every year afterward.*

This test may, at first sight, seem a lot of trouble to undertake. But is not 25 percent per annum of your advertising appropriation worth that trouble?

And what is it worth to know conclusively for all time the relative value of general publicity as actually compared with reason-why advertising in a downright selling test?

A difference of 66 percent between two such kinds of copy on equivalent tests has often been proved.

Isn't that a sufficient difference to make you sit up and think hard about what fills the space you pay for monthly?

A DIFFERENCE OF 66 PERCENT BETWEEN TWO SUCH KINDS OF COPY ON EQUIVALENT TESTS HAS OFTEN BEEN PROVED.

APPLYING REASON WHY ADVERTISING TO YOUR MODERN BUSINESS

Take a few moments to read the following prompts and write out your plan for effective advertising.

Salesmanship on Paper: *How can you ensure that your advertising acts as a salesperson, providing clear and compelling reasons for customers to buy?*

Proof Over Opinion: *What methods can you use to test and measure the effectiveness of your advertising rather than relying on assumptions?*

The Cost of Bad Advertising: *How can you evaluate whether your current advertising efforts are generating actual sales rather than just visibility?*

The Responsive Chord: *What are the strongest emotional and logical triggers that resonate with your target audience, and how can you incorporate them into your messaging?*

Targeting the Right Audience: *How can you refine your advertising strategy to focus on the people who need and can afford your product or service?*

Copy That Sells: *What specific reasons can you give potential customers to choose your product over competitors?*

Avoiding Trend-Based Advertising Mistakes: *How can you balance innovation in marketing with proven advertising principles that consistently drive sales?*

Positioning Your Brand for Success: *How can you clearly differentiate your brand in a way that makes it more appealing to customers?*

Tracking Advertising ROI: *What key metrics should you track to determine the actual return on investment (ROI) of your advertising campaigns?*

The Power of A/B Testing: *How can you implement A/B testing in your marketing efforts to determine what resonates most with your audience?*

Avoiding Blind Faith in General Publicity: *How can you ensure that every dollar spent on advertising contributes directly to business growth?*

Ad Copy vs. Sales Conversations: *What strategies can you use to make your written advertising as persuasive and compelling as a great face-to-face sales pitch?*

Making Every Ad Count: *How can you optimize your advertising strategy to maximize its effectiveness with the least amount of wasted effort?*

_____

_____

_____

_____

_____

_____

_____

_____

_____

_____

_____

_____

_____

_____

_____

_____

_____

_____

Turning Curiosity into Conviction: *How can you structure your advertising to not only attract attention but also convince potential buyers to take action?*

The Role of Trust in Advertising: *What elements can you incorporate into your advertising to build credibility and ensure customers trust your claims?*

The Power of Long-Term Consistency: *How can you develop a strong, consistent message that builds momentum over time and strengthens your brand's impact?*

ABOUT JOHN E. KENNEDY

John E. Kennedy (1864–1928) was a pioneering advertising copywriter. In 1904, Kennedy began working with Albert Lasker at the Chicago office of the advertising firm Lord & Thomas, where he became the highest-paid copywriter in all of advertising. Kennedy left Lord & Thomas after two years to start his own business, and in 1907 he became a principal at Edthridge-Kennedy Company in New York.

The history of advertising could never be written without first place in it being given to John E. Kennedy. The principles he laid down still shaped the world of advertising in the 20th century.

THINK & GROW RICH

BE PREPARED! When you expose yourself
to the influence of this philosophy, you
may experience a CHANGED LIFE!

This edition of Napoleon Hill's classic *Think and Grow Rich* is a reproduction of Napoleon Hill's personal copy of the first edition, the original version recommended by The Napoleon Hill Foundation, originally printed in March of 1937.

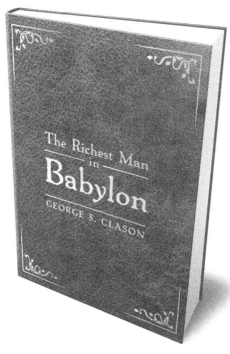

THANK YOU FOR READING THIS BOOK!

If you found any of the information helpful, please take a few minutes and leave a review on the bookselling platform of your choice.

BONUS GIFT!

Don't forget to sign up to try our newsletter and grab your free personal development ebook here:

soundwisdom.com/classics

Made in United States
Orlando, FL
28 August 2025

64381790R00075